P9-DHI-770

THAT
SHOULD
BE A
WORD

THAT SHOULD BE A WORD

A Language Lover's Guide to
Choregasms, Povertunity,
Brattling, and 250 Other
Much-Needed Terms for
the Modern World

LIZZIE SKURNICK

Illustrations by Janne Iivonen

WORKMAN PUBLISHING · NEW YORK

Copyright © 2015 by Lizzie Skurnick

Illustrations copyright © by Janne Iivonen

All rights reserved. No portion of this book may be reproduced—mechanically, electronically, or by any other means, including photocopying—without written permission of the publisher. Published simultaneously in Canada by Thomas Allen & Son Limited.

Library of Congress Cataloging-in-Publication Data is available.

ISBN 978-0-7611-8268-9

Design by Sarah Smith

Workman books are available at special discounts when purchased in bulk for premiums and sales promotions as well as for fund-raising or educational use. Special editions or book excerpts also can be created to specification. For details, contact the Special Sales Director at the address below, or send an email to specialmarkets@workman.com.

Workman Publishing Company, Inc.
225 Varick Street
New York, NY 10014-4381

workman.com

Workman is a registered trademark of Workman Publishing Co., Inc.

Printed in the United States of America
First printing March 2015

10 9 8 7 6 5 4 3 2 1   .

For Javier, who can only say "cat"

INTRODUCTION

I T IS A STANDING JOKE AMONG MY FRIENDS that not one of us got the joke of the restaurant "Nacho Mama's" before we were in our twenties. I also count significant delays in picking up on the following: a local restaurant called "The Barge Inn" that I had pegged as nautical; the double entendre of TV's *Queer as Folk*; numerous NPR shows (though why did they never use *As it Happens*?); the movie *Just Cause*; and hair salons beyond number. (Tress for Success! I got that one right away.)

It's no coincidence, of course, that puns, rhymes, and double (or triple) meanings abound in places that want to be welcoming. It's hard to find a title in a magazine that's *not* wordplay. That's because a title or name serves as an introduction—literally, a welcoming sign—suggesting that the people who propose to provide your reading matter; serve you their strange food; cut your hair; and tell you dire news on war, GMO's, and indie bands are not only funny, but that they can make fun of themselves. (DARPA, on the other hand, is not called "The Gunderminer.")

When I started churning out entries for *The New York Times Magazine* column "That Should Be a Word," readers sought not only wordplay but words about obscure feelings that nonetheless loomed large: a chocolate-chip cookie that turns out to be raisin (*bitrayal*); the slew of child-related media (*bornography*); the family member who always has to fix the computer (*domestech*). A story began to emerge: There was food (*Ingestigation*), marriage (*Martyrmony*), identity (*Mespoke*), emotion (*Dramaneering*), tech (*Fidgital*), work and money (*Bangst*), each deserving of its own chapter—subjects that already fattened dictionaries but nonetheless needed more words to fully describe them.

And it's this multiplicity—one word that melds other words into something greater than its parts—that makes a good neologism both a necessity and a joy. Neologisms are words we scrape up from existing words to reflect our own many-layered behavior, how our behavior and lives have intertwined in unexpected ways.

In this book you'll see how these words themselves tell a story of our culture. (Some words like "sentiyentl," the feeling of hearing an old Barbra Streisand song, were a bit too specific.) I've no doubt we could find even more cultural trends for expansion: gaming; horticulture; sports; organized crime; and other areas I know nothing about. There's an entire book for the names IKEA products actually *should* be called, I'm sure. But words, after all, are a conversation. I leave that to you.

THAT
SHOULD
BE A
WORD

(born-AH-gruh-fee), n.

The vast media content about child rearing.

"Ben and Enzo became bornography addicts, trolling buy buy BABY, signing up for alerts at babycenter.com, and subscribing to *Parents* magazine when they found out they were becoming grandfathers."

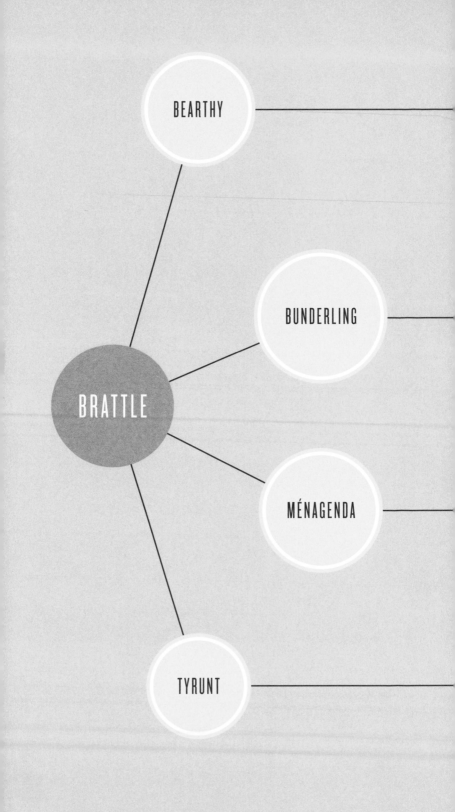

BEARTHY

BUNDERLING

BRATTLE

MÉNAGENDA

TYRUNT

PRAMBIVALENCE
KINNOVATOR

PREGMATIC
CLANARCHIST
INDIEPREGNANT

INFRANCY
PACIFIRE

DRIAPER
CRAWDLE
WHIMPALE
WHIMPERIL

GESTITUTION

SHPITZ
LICKTIM

INVERTEBRAT
DRAFTERBIRTH

NIPSTER
MOMBLE
DADAGE

BRATTLE

(BRAT-ul), v.

To discuss one's children, often at length. Also, such a discussion, n.

"Once the stroller comparisons rose to a fever pitch, Janki fled the living room to avoid the cocktail brattle."

TYRUNT

(TIE-runt), n.

Child who bosses everyone around.

"Jolene wondered whether it was the long-ago nursing-on-demand or her acceding to Beatrice's wish for a race-car bed that had made Beatrice such a tyrunt."

BEARTHY
(BUR-thee), adj.

Promoting natural birth.

"Eulalia had always thought she'd want to be knocked out the whole time, but she surprised herself by being a bearthy mom-to-be, purchasing a pool for her home delivery and deciding to plant the placenta under a specially chosen tree."

BUNDERLING
(BUN-der-ling), n.

New parent's role.

"Thinking of his endless nights consumed by bottles and changes, Max could not believe his ideal image of the ruling father was so far from the bunderling he'd become."

INFRANCY
(IN-frin-see), n.

Time when child can indicate desires but cannot speak.

"During her infrancy, Olivia's parents finally realized she laughed hysterically when she was tired and yawned theatrically when she was ready to eat."

PRAMBIVALENCE

(pram-BIV-uh-lents), n.

Unsureness about wanting children.

"Elizabeth was embarrassed to admit that it was an episode of *The Real Housewives of Beverly Hills* that finally ended her prambivalence and made her decide to have a kid."

KINNOVATOR

(KIN-o-vay-ter), n.

One who forms an untraditional family.

"John and Jack thought they were the best kinnovators when they adopted a girl from Vietnam, until they met Saul, who, as a single dad, had fostered enough children from five continents for a basketball team."

PACIFIRE *(PASS-ih-fire), n.*

The initial circle of hell of parenthood.

"At six months, Allegra looked up and found herself showered, her child dressed, and three bottles in the fridge. She'd come through the pacifire."

MÉNAGENDA

(mane-uh-JEN-duh), n.
Kid-driven family schedule.

"Mom learned that morning that the
ménagenda included a soccer game two hours
away, and then taking the whole team to
McDonald's."

PREGMATIC

(preg-MAT-ick), adj.

Doing childbirth by the book(s).

"Her friends tried to sell her on a lactation consultant, doula, and six-week baby nurse, but single working mom Masha was pregmatic: She'd try nursing for two weeks; have a friend be her birth partner; and live with Mom and Dad until she got on her feet."

CLANARCHIST *(KLAN-ar-kist), n.*

One who refuses traditional definitions of family.

"Perrie felt weird about living with his mother at 45, until he realized he was happy, got over it, and started calling himself a clanarchist instead of a loser."

INDIEPREGNANT

(in-dee-PREG-nint), adj.

Single mom-to-be.

"Tired of everyone asking whether her nonexistent husband wanted a boy or a girl, Tina started leading convos with, 'I'm indiepregnant!' before anyone could even offer congrats."

GESTITUTION

(jest-ih-TOO-shun), n.

What occurs when a child finally becomes a parent.

"When Soledad hung up the phone after comforting her hysterical daughter about toilet training, she breathed a sigh of satisfaction. Finally, gestitution!"

DRIAPER *(DRY-per), n.*

Diaper that didn't need changing.

"Wilson finally confronted Casey and told her she was going to bankrupt them if she kept throwing out driapers."

CRAWDLE *(CRAWD-ul), v.*

Be slow to walk.

"Lurlene was worried about Luke's crawdling well into his second year, until her brother asked her how many five-year-olds she knew that couldn't actually walk."

WHIMPALE *(wim-PAIL), v.*

Force to remain frozen by threat of crying.

"Hart found himself whimpaled on the landing outside the nursery for 30 minutes every night, until Sadia's deep breathing assured him that his 20 minutes of rocking had finally done the job."

WHIMPERIL *(wim-PEH-ril), v.*

Risk waking child with movement.

"It took Harriet only two days to realize that if she didn't get a binky into the baby's mouth *as* she removed the bottle, she was whimperiling the whole procedure."

INVERTEBRAT

(in-VERT-uh-brat), n.

Annoying offspring of clueless parents.

"What did the father think—that his invertebrat *wasn't* going to throw a huge tantrum if he brought him face-level with a bunch of donuts at Starbucks?"

DRAFTERBIRTH

(DRAF-ter-berth), n.

Children taken to bars.

"Crammed nightly with strollers and toddlers underfoot, the bar finally banned the parents' drafterbirth by making 18 the minimum age for entry."

SHPITZ *(SHPITS), v.*

Clean another's face with saliva.

"By age 8, Martha had become a skilled ducker when her grandmother licked her fingers to start shpitzing her."

LICKTIM *(LIK-tim), n.*

Person thus cleaned.

"Martha's brother Matt, with his dirty, fat, adorable cheeks, was Grandma's constant licktim."

NIPSTER *(NIP-ster), n.*

Baby hipster.

"Mirabelle's neighbors dressed their nipster with such irony that she wasn't sure if the vintage rain boots were utilitarian or some comment on *The Umbrellas of Cherbourg*."

MOMBLE *(MOM-bul), v.*

To mutter in answer to your parents or other adults.

"Anthony was told he'd be grounded if he mombled at his uncle one more time."

DADAGE *(DAD-ij), n.*

An old saw about fatherhood.

"Every time Bruce yanked out some old dadage from *Father Knows Best*, Merilee countered with 'The sins of the fathers.'"

(MAR-tir-moh-nee), n.

State of marriage that persists purely out of duty.

"Laurent wanted peace; Giselle wanted excitement—instead, they got shared, solid martyrmony."

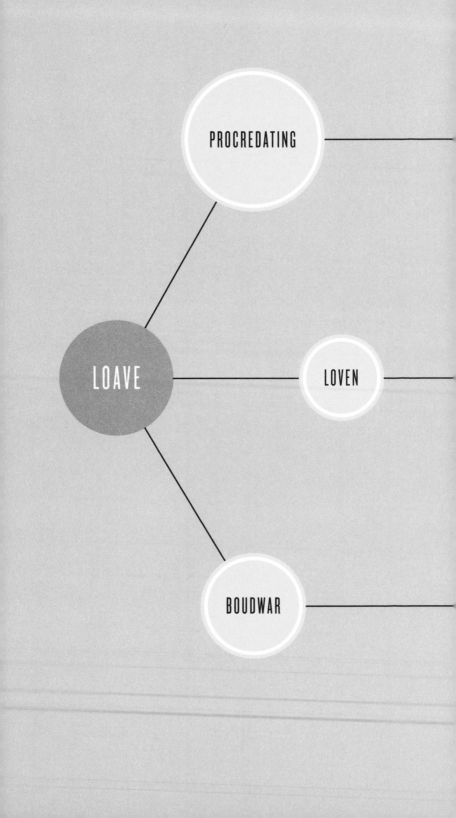

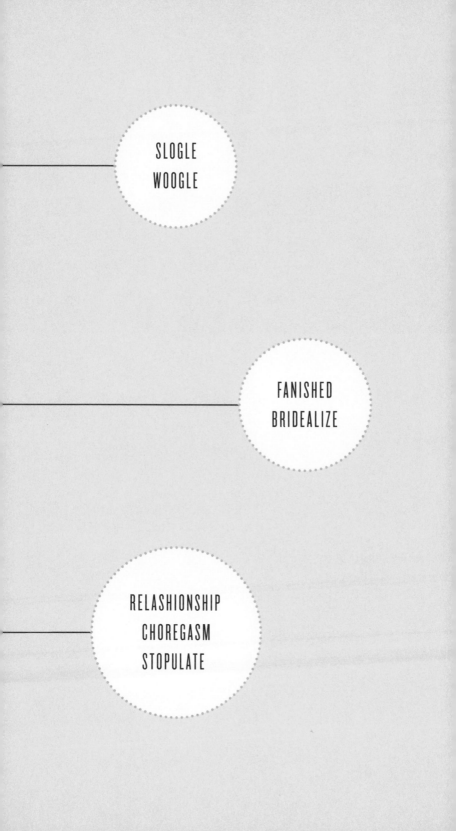

SLOGLE
WOOGLE

FANISHED
BRIDEALIZE

RELASHIONSHIP
CHOREGASM
STOPULATE

LOAVE

(LOHV), v.
To love and hate in equal proportions.

"Janice both trembled with anticipation and became flushed with rage the moment she saw Adella: She loaved her."

BOUDWAR *(boo-DWORE), n.*

An argument originating in the bedroom.

"Don thought the boudwar began when he didn't kiss Estelle good night. Little did he know it had started that morning, when he left the bed unmade."

PROCREDATING

(PRO-kree-day-ting), v.

Actively looking for a partner to start a family with.

"At first, it was embarrassing to be procredating, but by the time Flora and Hugo met and fell in love, they'd both realized it was more efficient to simply say they were planning on having at least five kids and clear the field."

LOVEN

(LUV-in), *n.*

A superheated amour.

"Marijane and Edouard's loven stretched from June to October, when they woke up and realized it was too chilly to simply walk around naked anymore."

SLOGLE *(SLOW-gull), v.*

Reduce one's speed in order to catcall.

"Archie thought slogling and yelling at hot babes was a sign of warmth and virility until Samuel informed him it was kind of gross."

WOOGLE *(WOO-gull), v.*

Curry favor by posting flattering content of one's self online for prospective searchers.

"Brian uploaded some pictures of himself ladling gravy at a soup kitchen when he set out to woogle his do-gooder coworker."

FANISHED *(FAN-isht), adj.*

Starving post-sex.

"Jean had no idea what John's favorite part of amorous relations was, but hers was when they were fanished and ate all the junk food he had at his house."

BRIDEALIZE *(BRY-dee-uh-lize), v.*

To go overboard on planning a wedding.

"When it occurred to Patrice she'd spent almost three hours downloading old episodes of *Say Yes to the Dress* to find a good hairstyle to go with her tiara, she realized she was actually bridealizing."

RELASHIONSHIP

(ree-LASH-un-ship), n.
Bad romance you can't leave.

"Bo ran into her old business partner Bob at a car show and was shocked to find she and he could chat happily—despite his making off with the company's profits and her changing the locks on their fully stocked warehouse ages ago, they clearly hadn't had enough of their relashionship."

CHOREGASM

(CHORE-gazz-um), n.
A tedious finish.

"From hot sex to choregasm in 100 days? That must have been what plagued Anne Boleyn and Henry Tudor, a slightly impassioned scholar decided."

STOPULATE *(STOP-you-late), v.*

To halt midcoitus to declare terms.

"Five minutes in, Pam stopulated that they were never to use the term *love* until they were really, really sure it was."

DRAMANEERING

(drah-muh-NEAR-ing), adj.

Maintaining control by seeming to be in crisis.

"To get his way, Noel's dramaneering boyfriend routinely deployed slow weeping, followed by book-hurling, knowing that by the time he got to the crouching-by-the-refrigerator part, she would give in."

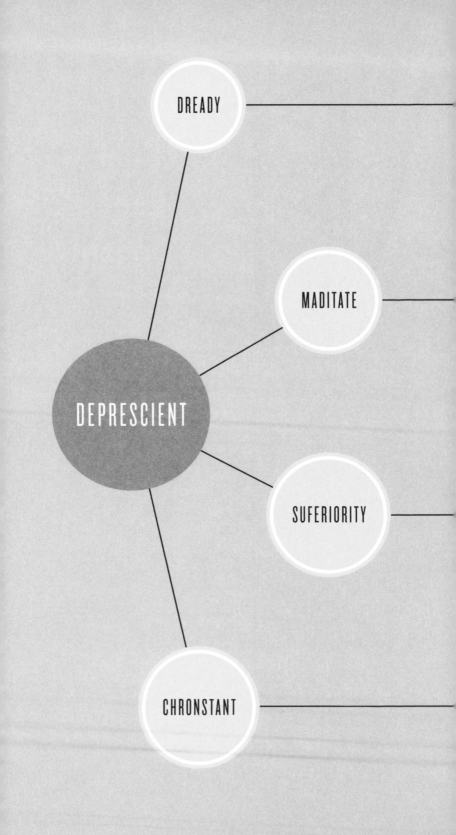

SADDICT
SHALTERED

WORIGINS
DUNCERTAIN
PARALASSIST

IMPARIOUS
IMPLACTICAL
SLUMBRAGE

MOROSY
RECRITIVISM

BLUPHORIA
LOSTENTATIOUS
CANVICT
SOBTIMIST

RELIABAIL
STARDY
CANTICIPATE

DEPRESCIE

(duh-PRESH-int), adj.

Imagining the worst will happen.

"Giran sat home on Sundays and canned jams for his lone survival of the apocalypse: typical deprescient behavior."

NT

MADITATE

(MAD-it-ate), v.
Become angrier by trying to calm down.

"Taking deep breaths and trying to think how she could have negotiated getting her raise more effectively, Janine instead found herself maditating on her undermining, unappreciative boss."

SUFERIORITY

(sue-fear-ee-OR-ih-tee), n.
Ego masking insecurity.

"Crippled by suferiority, Pasie could only manage to seem confident on the first round of Trivial Pursuit before she started second-guessing herself and losing."

DREADY

(DRED-ee), adj.

Always prepared for disaster.

"As she pulled out the spare bottle from the diaper bag, Gloria thanked god her husband was so dready."

CHRONSTANT

(KRON-stint), adj.

Always on time.

"Pat, militantly chronstant, could not believe that her best friend, who worked as a bus driver on a busy route, liked to go with her 'internal rhythm' rather than wear a watch."

SADDICT *(SAD-ikt), n.*

One who thrives on misery.

"Lyndon tried everything to cheer his Mom—giving her flowers, cleaning his room, changing his socks—but by high school he'd concluded she was a die-hard saddict."

SHALTERED *(SHALL-terd), adj.*

Innocently credulous.

"When she moved to the city, Judith was so shaltered she still obeyed her grandmother's admonition to always cross her legs at the ankles until her roommate pointed out she was actually tripping people on the subway."

IMPARIOUS

(im-PAIR-ee-us), adj.

Confidently leading in the wrong direction.

"Imparious to the last, the CEO invested all the company's resources in fracking, which went out of style after all clean water dried up and the planet was reduced to a beer-swigging dystopia."

IMPLACTICAL

(im-PLAK-tik-ul), adj.

Strong in the face of extreme unlikeliness.

"Implactical Lawrence submitted the same essay to *The New Yorker* over and over, reasoning that within the decade it would have to arrive on the desk of an editor who adored it."

SLUMBRAGE *(SLUM-brij), n.*

Slow-to-grow anger.

"It didn't help that Luba's slumbrage took as long as three months to emerge, leaving her sister at a loss as to what she was even talking about."

WORIGINS *(WOR-uh-jins), n.*

Source of a mysterious anxiety.

"Being knocked over by a dog at 8; breaking a mirror at 10; peeing on a bus at 12—David tried to let go of his own worigins and let his son go away to camp."

DUNCERTAIN *(dun-SER-tin), adj.*

Unsure if one has completed a task.

"Filled with duncertainty, Alex finally went home on his lunch hour to check the burner."

PARALASSIST

(puh-RAL-uh-sist), n.

Freezing up when help is required.

"Marta finally overcame her paralassist the day some teenagers began to bait an old man on a bus: She found that having a large umbrella gave her a big mouth."

MOROSY

(muh-ROH-zee), adj.

Concealing sadness with cheer.

"It was not until she came upon her roommate weeping in the bathroom minutes after she'd happily agreed to go to Pinkberry that Estelle realized poor Sandrine was tragically morosy."

RECRITIVISM

(ree-CRIT-uh-viz-um), n.

Torturous preoccupation with long-ago mistakes.

"The therapist tried to help the couple through their recritivism: Yes, the part where the husband threw half his wife's shoes out and she cut all his ties in half had been a low moment, but they did not have to return to it every time the toaster wasn't working."

RELIABAIL *(ree-LYE-uh-bale), adj.*

Always canceling.

"After perennially reliabail Craig stuck Jordan with two $600 Springsteen tickets after they'd agreed on the date for months, he deleted him from his cell phone."

STARDY *(STAR-dee), adj.*

Setting off late.

"Gene learned to tell his stardy wife, Blanche, that a party began two hours earlier than the invitation specified, just so they had a fighting chance to get there before it ended."

CANTICIPATE *(can-TISS-ih-pate), v.*

To visualize negative events or consequences.

"For two days before her speech, Rachel canticipated freezing, losing her place, and generally bombing, such that she couldn't eat a thing, went to the stage light-headed, and fainted."

BLUPHORIA *(bloo-FOR-ee-uh), n.*

Happiness that sparks melancholy.

"Mary Kate was filled with bluphoria at the end of her favorite series, *The Chronicles of Narnia*, knowing she'd never read it for the first time again."

LOSTENTATIOUS

(loss-ten-TAY-shuss), adj.

Overly public about one's downfall.

"In terms of being lostentatious, Salvatore and Hilda were in a standoff: While he trumpeted his lack of a job with a Tumblr of things he'd been forced to sell, she'd recently completed a memoir of her perfectly happy childhood that nonetheless detailed numerous travails."

CANVICT *(CAN-vikt), n.*

One imprisoned by inability to say no.

"Diana might be such a canvict she was booked every weekend for the next two months, but Artemis had no trouble blithely blowing off whatever inane commitment her wife had agreed to."

SOBTIMIST *(SOB-tih-mist), n.*

One who cries over good fortune.

"Terry's sobtimism came out every time she looked at the rare book collection left to her by her father, knowing she'd finish them . . . someday."

THERATROOPER

INSTABORDINATE

GLEEVIL

SLOWTH

AMIGRATE
PALBATROSS

COMREADS
DUMPIRE
CHUMBRAGE

GRISCHIEF
THAUGHTY

CHARMAMENT
INDAMNIFY
RATIONALIES

OUGHTY
PLASSITUDE
PLEISURE

INSTABOR

(IN-stuh-BORE-dih-net), adj.
Reflexively disobedient.

"Trip was so instabordinate he was unable to keep from whispering 'Jerkoff' as his boss walked by."

GLEEVIL

(GLEE-vul), adj.

Happily disobedient.

"Marc tried to feel bad as his mother upbraided him for filling his brother's shoes with chunks of Jell-O, but even after being caught, he couldn't help but be gleevil about the whole thing."

SLOWTH

(SLOHTH), n.

Ever-increasing lassitude.

"Consumed by slowth, Craig wrote ten pages of his thesis one day, five the next, and by the next week had cycled down to two words an hour."

DINATE →

THERATROOPER

(THEH-ruh-troo-per), n.

Friend who swoops in to commiserate.

"Therese had to admit she actually loved the role of theratrooper—Dante's weekly crises brought a spot of color into her currently very dull life."

GRISCHIEF *(GRISS-chif), n.*

Material used for misbehavior.

"Six pineapples, an abandoned bicycle, approaching dusk: Was there ever better grischief for a 12-year-old?"

THAUGHTY *(THAW-tee), adj.*

Guilty of saucy imaginings.

"Thank god Django was only thaughty: He was sure if he'd actually brought a tub of Cool Whip and suggested they go to town, his matchmaker's choice would have left him that night."

AMIGRATE *(AM-ih-grate), v.*

To move from one friendship to another.

"When Fantine began amigrating to Brea, Zoe never tried to sell a friend on another friend again."

PALBATROSS *(PAL-buh-tross), n.*

A friend you'd like to drop.

"Chuck was convinced that Brea was a palbatross until their mutual friend Zoe showed him that Brea was actually making very funny jokes; she just said them so low they were hard to hear. But then he got annoyed at that."

COMREADS (COM-reedz), n.

People who read a book at the same time.

"Jen and her comreads regretted choosing the endless *The Man Without Qualities*."

DUMPIRE (DUM-pyre), n.

Person who has to hear both sides of a fight.

"The worst part of being the dumpire, Keld thought, was reassuring both members of an angry couple, knowing they were both going to be pissed and blow him off once they got back together."

CHUMBRAGE (CHUM-brij), n.

Irritation on a friend's behalf.

"George was filled with chumbrage every time Mack's father yelled at his friend, but he was too young to do anything about it."

CHARMAMENT

(CHAR-ma-ment), n.

An arsenal of weapons of seduction.

"June felt flattered by Bill's near-assault of affections and interest, until she realized he released his charmaments on anyone."

INDAMNIFY *(in-DAM-nih-fye), v.*

Adjust behavior to avoid criticism.

"Parson began to indamnify himself against their usual fight over his coming home late by texting his wife a picture of his overloaded desk."

RATIONALIES

(RASH-un-uh-lyz), n.

Justifications of falsehoods.

"By the time Marcus had purchased a yacht to go with the slip rental that went with the captain's hat that went with his new deck shoes, his rationalies had put him into serious debt."

THAT SHOULD BE A WORD

OUGHTY *(AW-tee), adj.*

Guilty but lazy anyhow.

"Slim watched the giant pile of laundry loom larger from across the room as she fired up the TiVo, her feet buried under a couch cushion in oughty repose."

PLASSITUDE *(PLAS-ih-tood), n.*

Laziness without guilt.

"His father's admonitions that if he never turned in his homework on time he would wind up a starving bum on the street were not enough to deter Michel from his plassitude."

PLEISURE *(PLEE-zhur), n.*

Joy of doing nothing.

"George replaced the severe Eames chair in his summer house with a Barcalounger to attain maximum pleisure."

(DRONE-ah-niz-um), n.

Love of hearing oneself talk.

"Pearl learned to despise her dronanist husband and frequently sent him out gardening, lest she be subject to yet another musing on whatever he'd recently read in *The Atlantic*."

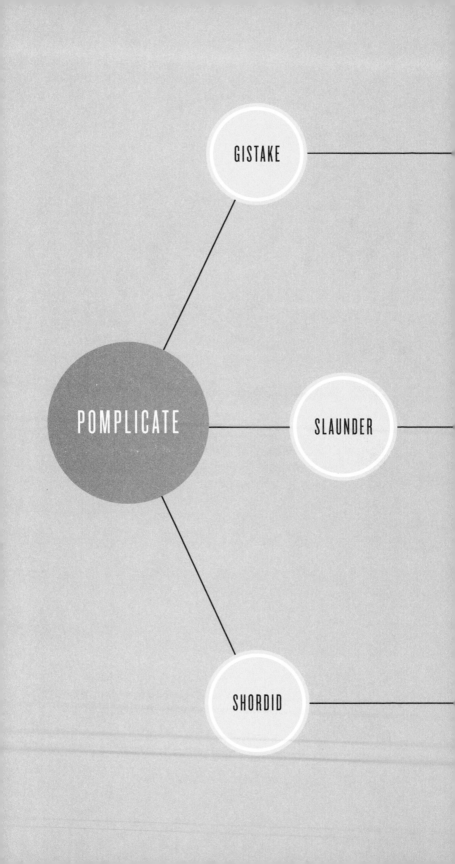

SPEECHIOUS
DICTAPLANARIAN

CHARMALADE
CLUCID
SPELLOT
WIRGIN

DENIGREET
QUASHTION
TRUIN

FLAWSOME
NEQUESSITY
EFFUSAL

GAFFTERMATH
FRANKLE

HORIDAY
WORDURE
WRONGLE

POMPLICA

(POM-pli-kate), v.

To create unnecessary confusion with formality.

"Jo had to get her seatmate to translate her professor, who could pomplicate an absolutely obvious point with three or four S.A.T. words."

TE

SLAUNDER

(SLAWN-der), v.

To pass gossip through several sources so it cannot be traced to you.

"Sally liked to slaunder tidbits through Regina, who couldn't keep secrets and usually got them from several sources."

SHORDID

(SHOR-did), adj.

Confessed scandal.

"After his third acknowledgment of using the public coffers to support his foot fetish–DVD addiction, Pam finally left her husband and their shordid past behind."

GISTAKE (jis-TAKE), n.

Incorrect word that still gets the point across.

"Coach's speech was peppered with gistakes like *blockage* and *defendance* and *mightivate*, but his loyal team always understood him completely."

SPEECHIOUS (SPEE-chiss), adj.

Obscure, meaningless, and lengthy.

"Maestro Anderson's speechious rants always went unchallenged, as his orchestra was too fatigued to even object with logic by the time he was done."

DICTAPLANARIAN

(DICK-tuh-pluh-NARE-ee-yun), n.

Enforcer of correct pronunciation.

"Dictaplanarian Jody could always be counted on to say *err* was actually pronounced 'urr,' particularly in a group and when it was most embarrassing to the speaker."

CHARMALADE *(CHARM-uh-laid), n.*

Deftness in luring someone into bed.

"Luellen and Gilles were both masters of charmalade, but found when they met that neither needed to even seduce the other."

CLUCID *(KLOO-sid), adj.*

Hinting instead of saying.

"Mrs. Lyles was the most clucid teacher Carmine had ever had—she seemed to feel that every hint about 'national nightmare' and 'crook' was as obvious to the class as it was to her."

SPELLOT *(SPEL-ut), n.*

One who takes red pen to all documents.

"Dirk stopped sending emails to his spellot daughter, since she would constantly send them back with the mistakes corrected."

WIRGIN *(WUR-jin), n.*

One who has yet to cuss.

"Alice shocked her sorority sisters when she dropped a punch bowl and screamed, 'Fuck!' She had been their house's only wirgin."

DENIGREET *(DEN-uh-greet), v.*

Pretend never to have met.

"After the fourth time Clunie denigreeted Maud, the latter just started introducing herself as Claude."

QUASHTION *(KWASH-chunn), n.*

Rhetorical "no."

"The policewoman's sentence was a flat quashtion: 'If I didn't give *you* a ticket, how would I explain that to everyone else I gave a ticket to today?'"

TRUIN *(TROO-in), v.*

Demolish a long-held belief with facts.

"Andrès was thrilled when thrill-seekers began using a variation of wings to cliff-dive, as Esmé was always truining his plans by citing various principles of physics as he worked on his feathered prototype."

GAFFTERMATH *(GAF-ter-math), n.*

Fallout from a scandal.

"In the gafftermath of his praising Kansas for the fine Kansas City barbecue, Senator Mars was forced to eat his way through ten plates of ribs and buy T-shirts with maps of Missouri for his whole staff."

FRANKLE *(FRANK-ul), v.*

To annoy someone by telling the truth.

"Margalit frankled her sister Isolde so deeply by declaring her macrame purse an abomination, Isolde sent her a $5 Old Navy gift certificate for her birthday."

FLAWSOME *(FLAW-sum), adj.*

Equally complimentary and insulting.

"Which praise was more flawsome? The time Adelle's BFF told her she looked way better than she had in months, or when her teacher mentioned that she was surprised by how well Adelle had done on the final?"

NEQUESSITY *(neh-KWES-ih-tee), n.*

Order phrased as question.

"For the first year of their marriage, Johan's husband, Tom, refused his brother-in-law's request to stand in the back row of the family photo, until a vigorous nudge from the exasperated Tom made him finally realize it wasn't family hospitality, it was a nequessity."

EFFUSAL *(eh-FUSE-ill), n.*

Art of saying no by seeming overly pleased.

"After three months in the genteel South, Babette finally realized her neighbors' cheery promises to come by sometime were actually effusal, and they would never be free for any of her Mary Kay parties."

HORIDAY *(HOAR-uh-day), n.*

A less than stellar celebration.

"Yuri adored the organic veggies of the summer and winter solstices, but the rest of the year was full of unhealthy horidays—cheap, chocolaty Easters; sticky, candy-licking Christmases; dense, heart-clogging, matzo-balled Passovers."

WORDURE *(WER-jer), n.*

Statements full of shit.

"When Albert started regaling his younger neighbors about how great life was for men in the good old days, his wife, Helen, was always there to stave off his stream of wordure."

WRONGLE *(RONG-gull), v.*

To convince someone to do something by finessing the truth.

"A cruise on the line that had just had a flu outbreak on its ships was not a 'bargain,' Joseph realized. His alumni organization had wrongled him into attending for the last time."

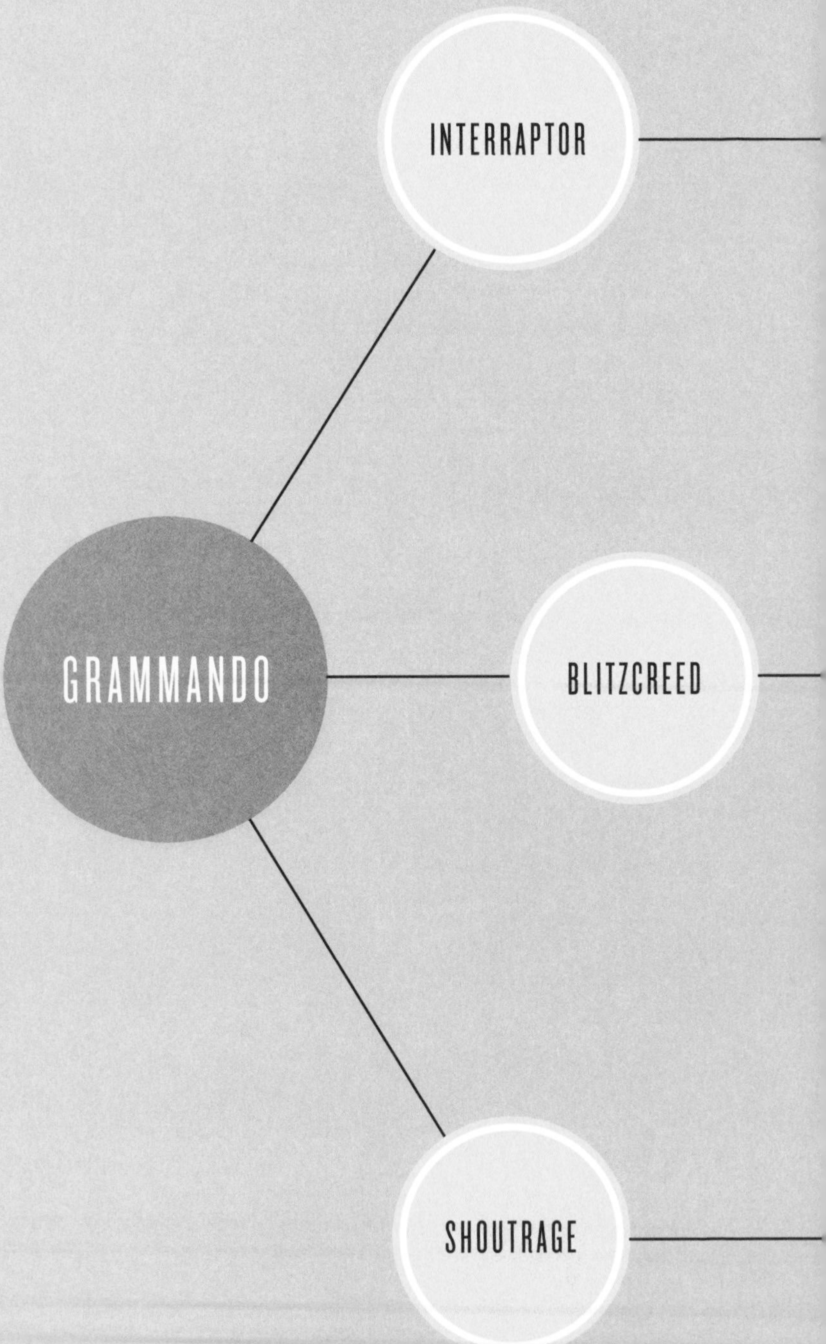

INTERRAPTOR

GRAMMANDO

BLITZCREED

SHOUTRAGE

NODINAGE
STORIS

AUTOPRYLOT
QUARY
FRADIO
SLOCAB

WORDITION
PESTION
MOPINE

GRUMPTION
CALMBAT

POUTRAGE
STORBEAR
DOUBTRAGE

GRAMMAN

(gruh-MAN-doh), adj.
Constantly correcting others' linguistic mistakes.

"Cowed by his grammando wife, Pankaj finally learned the difference between *that* and *which*."

SHOUTRAGE

(SHOUT-rayj), n.
Irate explosion.

"Janelle took to wearing earplugs in her kitchen, where she could nightly hear her upstairs neighbors' fits of shoutrage."

DO

INTERRAPTOR

(in-ter-RAP-ter), n.

One who cannot wait for other person to finish.

"Sally finally found a way to stop the interraptor—she jingled the ice in her gin and tonic every time she made a point, being sure to jingle it right in his face."

NODINAGE *(nod-ih-NAHZH), n.*

Shaking of one's head in agreement in lieu of speaking.

"Master of nodinage, Paulette actually managed to take a standing catnap at a particularly boring conference."

STORIS *(STORE-us), n.*

Anxiety about telling a joke or anecdote without losing the crowd.

"Stella's best friend always made her tell the one about the dog, the professor, and the lost cell phone, even though it filled her with storis to remember to put the phone before the dog."

BLITZCREED

(BLITS-kreed), n.
Trumpeting one's beliefs.

"James was tiring of the holiday blitzcreeds: the first, mass missives from friends told them all that without their $50, 400 children would go without food, or, that if they didn't install a composting toilet, global warming would never be conquered."

AUTOPRYLOT *(AW-tow-pry-lit)*, n.

Perfunctory questioning.

"Ruth realized she'd gone on autoprylot and quizzed Bertha about her job, love life, and favorite paint colors, all without hearing one reply."

QUARY *(KWAY-ree)*, n.

Tentative question.

"Modo followed up the aggressive answer from the president with a quary: 'Can I, um, ask one more question?'"

FRADIO *(FRAY-dee-oh)*, n.

One who fears being overheard.

"Marcus liked to mock his fradio sister by loudly repeating to the assembly anything she whispered to him."

SLOCAB *(SLOW-cab)*, n.

The words you can't think of.

"Rianna thought having mom brain was a myth until she started needing to pause for 20 seconds to let the slocab rise to the surface."

WORDITION *(wer-DISH-un), n.*

Being stuck around a person who won't stop talking.

"Paula always found faculty parties the worst kind of wordition."

PESTION *(PEST-shun), v.*

To ask something over and over.

"Marco was a master of the pestion, waiting until his parents had relaxed to strike up the 'When will we get there?' variations again."

MOPINE *(MOH-pyne), v.*

Muse on source of discontent.

"Even a bottle of fancy Maker's Mark wasn't enough to lure Jared to go to his bud's pad and listen to him mopine away another Saturday night."

GRUMPTION *(GRUMP-shun), n.*

Boldness born of irritation.

"Seeing only male authors' works in the front window of the bookstore filled the normally shy feminist Hector with grumption, and he switched the display to all women one night while the boss wasn't looking."

CALMBAT *(KAHM-bat), n.*

Unruffled argument.

"A rowdy studio audience had taught the host that calmbat was much more effective with them than counterattacking or being defensive."

POUTRAGE *(POUT-rage), n.*

Anger by way of whining.

"The babysitter was onto her new charge immediately: She could ignore the poutrage over getting no second ice-cream cone."

STORBEAR *(store-BEAR), v.*

To sustain aggrievement.

"Lillith knew she would have to storbear her gardener's son's treatment of her iris until his father, a gentle caretaker, returned from vacation."

DOUBTRAGE *(DOWT-rage), n.*

Uncertainty about whether one should be mad.

"River responded to his mother-in-law's needling of his son with doubtrage—was she just working through her undeniably tragic childhood? (And did it matter?)"

(in-JEST-uh-gay-shun), n., v.

Close examination of repast; to examine thus.

"Most campers just inhaled the vegan loaf, but Jordan ingestigated it carefully, making sure the green bits were actually kale and not something far more disturbing."

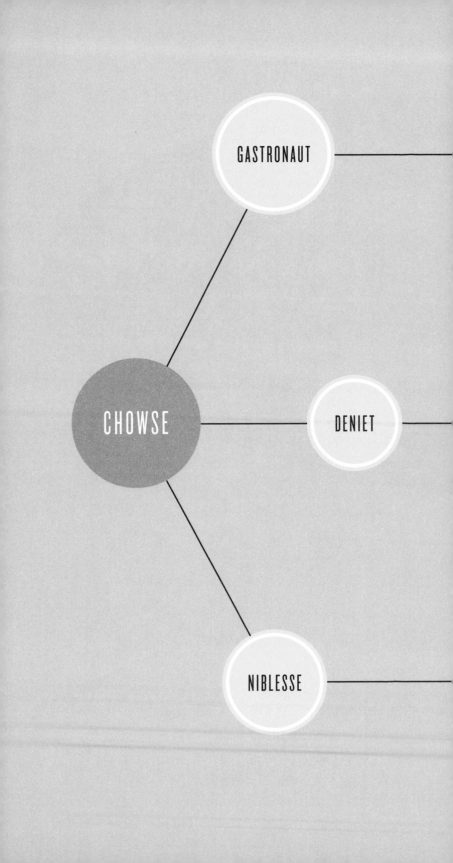

GASTRONAUT

CHOWSE

DENIET

NIBLESSE

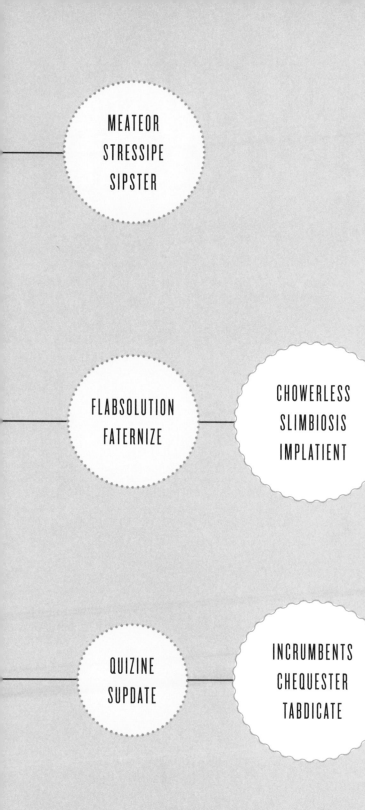

MEATEOR
STRESSIPE
SIPSTER

FLABSOLUTION
FATERNIZE

CHOWERLESS
SLIMBIOSIS
IMPLATIENT

QUIZINE
SUPDATE

INCRUMBENTS
CHEQUESTER
TABDICATE

CHOWSE

(CHOWZ), v.

Absentmindedly eat the food in one's vicinity.

"Meeting the in-laws was already awkward, but once Vera chowsed Betrand's penne, the meal was nigh unsalvageable."

NIBLESSE *(nib-LESS), n.*

Those who eat only exorbitantly priced foods.

"Tasting menus; wine pairings; croissants delivered from only one special bakery in the tri-state area: Scott was a prime member of the niblesse."

GASTRONAUT

(GAS-troh-nawt), *n.*

One on an out-there diet.

"Having invited two gastronauts to Thanksgiving dinner, June found herself trying to make a chocolate cake without any actual chocolate and ransacking Shop-Rite for something called millet."

DENIET *(duh-NYE-it)*, *n.*

Lie about cheating on regimen.

"After a week of 'just a taste' and 'skim ruins the crema,' Ludell's two-pound gain attested to an unequivocal deniet."

MEATEOR *(MEE-tee-or), n.*

Passing high-protein fad.

"When the recommendations switched back to veggies and pasta, Al was glad that he, unlike Stan, had chosen not to buy half of a cow during the latest meateor."

STRESSIPE *(STRES-ih-pee), n.*

A dish that's more trouble to cook than it's worth.

"Watching the Eastern European tea cakes he'd spent weeks to shop for and prepare correctly be gobbled in five minutes by his book group, Rob decided to avoid stressipes from now on."

SIPSTER *(SIPP-stir), n.*

One who expresses coolness through drinks.

"Thor was an inveterate sipster: He would argue over the merits of hand-poured coffee like it was an indie band."

FLABSOLUTION

(flab-suh-LOO-shun), n.

Self-forgiveness for weight gain.

"There must be a traveler's forgiveness for having clotted cream, roasted chicken, and churros in a single week. Zach felt flabsolution."

FATERNIZE

(FAT-ern-eyes), v.

Hang out with other unhealthy eaters.

"When he craved pulled pork, Steve chose to faternize with his midwestern coworker rather than try to convince his vegetarian family to go."

QUIZINE *(kwiz-EEN), n.*

Food that requires lengthy explanation.

"Since the restaurant's quizine included such keepers as 'fast-blown sherry,' 'wilted increase,' and 'foam precedent,' to amuse himself, Wils often brought along his non-English-speaking friends, who would not realize the phrases were ridiculous."

SUPDATE *(SUP-date), n.*

Food-related posting.

"Anika realized that her friends' supdates— glorious shots of pork belly confit, baby arugula salads, unidentifiable bottom-feeders—were simply the grown-up versions of the innumerable black-and-white shots of their bare feet with packs of cigarettes they'd taken in high school."

CHOWERLESS

(CHOW-ur-less), adj.

Enervated from lack of food.

"Henry could not believe they were taking so long to make him a lousy cheese sandwich, but he was chowerless and too close to fainting to even call the waiter over to complain."

SLIMBIOSIS

(slim-buy-OH-sis), n.

Feeling oneself shrink immediately upon joining a gym or purchasing lo-cal foods.

"As Serge considered asking the trim thirty-something b-ballers at the park if he could play, he felt himself regaining his pre-middle-aged musculature through a kind of slimbiosis."

IMPLATIENT

(im-PLAY-shent), adj.

Edgy for food to get on the table.

"When Piers realized his twins were so implatient they'd wander into the fridge for Go-gurts while he was basting the duck, he simply stopped cooking for them altogether."

INCRUMBENTS *(in-KRUM-bents), n.*

Dawdling diners.

"Nina was torn between peeing and staying in line, knowing that if she didn't pounce on the corner incrumbents' table, the twitchy couple with the laptops would."

CHEQUESTER *(cheh-QUEST-er), v.*

Seize the bill.

"Joan chequestered the scribbled total while her friend was in the restroom so she could make sure he didn't manage to put in even a tip on his birthday."

TABDICATE *(TAB-duck-ate), v.*

Let someone else figure out the check.

"Having made a vow to leave division and volleyball back in high school, Aimee happily tabdicated after-dinner drinks."

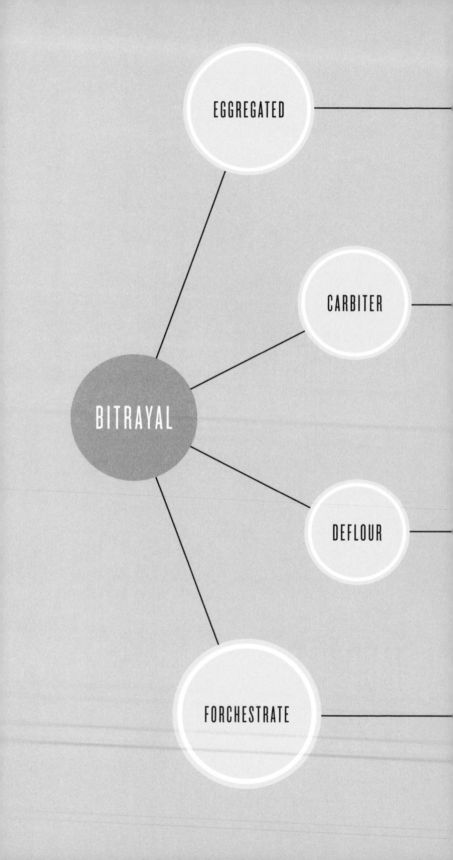

EGGREGATED

CARBITER

BITRAYAL

DEFLOUR

FORCHESTRATE

BRUEFUL
PLASTICATE

BITEMIZE
CARBITURATES

FASTRONOME
FEDITOR

CHEWSY
FOODGE

BITRAYAL

(bit-RAY-ul), n.

Emotion occasioned by biting into a foodstuff you thought was another flavor.

"Having suffered the bitrayal of raisin for chocolate-chip once too often, Rory sniffed all cookies prepurchase."

FORCHESTRATE

(FOR-keh-strayt), v.

To design a dish so that diner must eat an element of each item on plate in one bite.

"Lisa was advised that the chef had forchestrated her dish personally, so she should heap her fork with two chick peas, three microgreens, a dab of caviar, and a bread crumb in foamed sour cream."

CARBITER

(CAR-bit-er), n.

One who asserts that someone else cannot still be hungry.

"Beatrix was such an incurable carbiter, Piotr took to hiding Mallomars under the bed for desperate moments."

DEFLOUR

(dee-FLAU-err), v.

To strip a dish of all its carbohydrates.

"To stay on the Gwyneth Paltrow diet, Felicia defloured her quesadilla, peeling back the doughy carapace to fork out the safe, shredded chicken from the center."

EGGREGATED
(EG-ruh-gayt-d), adj.

With egg whites separated from yolks prior to cooking.

"Marcel's son would only eat eggregated quiche, making the final product, to his French father's dismay, the consistency of rubber and the color of Wonder Bread."

BITEMIZE
(BYE-tum-eyes), v.

Count calories.

"If he kept bitemizing her every breakfast, Prudence decided she was going to add prune juice to her father's coffee and see how he liked that."

CARBITURATES

(car-BIT-chew-ritz), n.

Addictive non-Atkins foodstuffs.

"The corner bakery was full of Dora's childhood carbiturates: poppy-seed rolls, kugel, and rows and rows of supersized cookies."

FASTRONOME

(FAST-ruh-nohm), adj.

Someone who asserts the value of cleanses.

"Brianna kept her head down whenever her fastronome parents took out the juicer, knowing that they'd be snapping at her by the third day even as they claimed they felt only more energetic, healthy, and clearheaded."

FEDITOR

(FED-ih-ter), n.

Someone who removes offending items from her meal.

"Had Dorcas known her new stepsister was such an ungrateful feditor, she never would have experimented with almonds in the salad."

BRUEFUL *(BROO-ful), adj.*

Feeling regret after drinking something you thought was something else.

"After swigging a cup of baby formula she'd expected to be soy milk, a brueful Rachel stayed away from all unidentified liquids."

PLASTICATE *(PLAS-tick-ate), v.*

Mistakenly bite fake fruit.

"A summer of working as an orderly and routinely plasticating shiny apples made Warren leery of all old-age homes."

CHEWSY *(CHOO-zee), adj.*

Likes or dislikes certain foods for texture alone.

"Mira rolled her eyes at her chewsy boyfriend Yossi, who could not even be near her while she ate her apparently disgustingly stringy snack of celery, but then happily ate all the steak gristle she left on the side of her dinner plate."

FOODGE *(FOOJ), v.*

To replace one ingredient with another.

"Lacking peanut butter or vanilla extract, Booker tried to foodge the peanut-butter cookies with ground almonds and a raspberry yogurt."

POVER

TUNITY

(pah-ver-TOON-uh-tee), n.

A job with more status than salary.

"Working for a production company for the chance to meet celebrities and free use of the craft table: It was the best povertunity Blaise had gotten in some time."

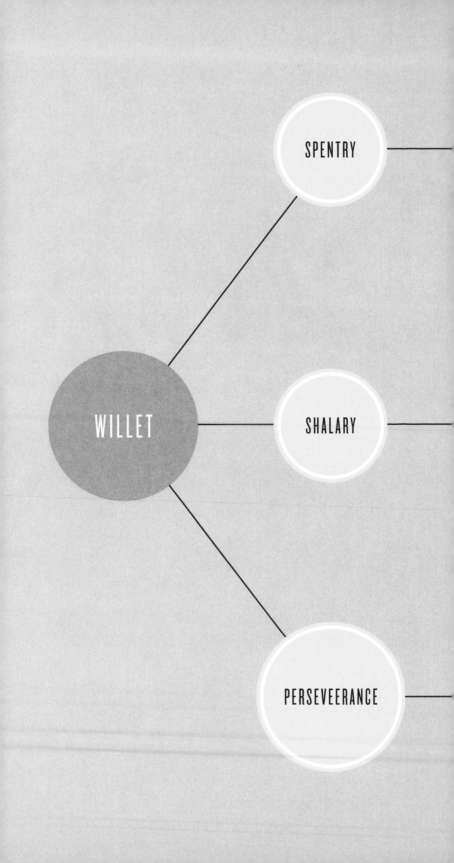

BUYCHOLOGY
GLAMORTIZE

CRAMBITIOUS
SNOOPERVISE

CLOUTRAGE
CUBICULL
DONELY

FAULTITASK
RESULTORY
CHOREFUL

WILLET

(WILL-et), *n.*

A plan for one's funds.

"Anthony's willet collapsed when the MTA began releasing limited-edition models of early trains—for half the sum of his rent."

SPENTRY

(SPEN-tree), n.

A class that lives beyond its means.

"The real estate broker felt gloomy looking at the abandoned McMansions of the spentry who were now underwater, even though he knew he was going to make a killing selling their echoing estates to foreign investors."

SHALARY

(SHALL-ah-ree), n.

Dangled raise.

"Dan was offered a shalary of 50 thousand a year, with a 10-thousand-dollar bonus if he learned Esperanto and brought in 20 international clients in the first three months."

BUYCHOLOGY *(bye-CALL-uh-jee), n.*

The science of making people make purchases.

"Kara didn't know who had figured out the buychology of having the candy below the check-out counter and the magazines to the left, but it worked: She found herself slapping down a Snickers with her *Us Weekly* every time."

GLAMORTIZE *(GLAM-er-tyes), v.*

Calculate how long it will take an expensive item to pay for itself.

"Pierce justified the purchase of the mink stole by glamortizing it—he would wear it the next 27 winters, he decided, making it only $75 a year."

PERSEVEERANCE

(PER-seh-VEER-ants), n.

Procrastination via performing other tasks.

"Troja's perseveerance caused her failure to complete her novel, but she did acquire a rock garden, a new bathroom floor, and a mastery of Asian fusion cuisine."

CRAMBITIOUS *(cram-BISH-us), adj.*

Taking on an excessive workload to advance in one's career.

"Bessie was crambitious enough to take a job consulting for Hampton Inns and start a waffle-maker line herself."

SNOOPERVISE *(SNOO-per-vize), v.*

Secretly monitor employees.

"A particularly obnoxious group of parents started to snoopervise the nannies in the park with actual cameras, letting other parents know if, god forbid, their babysitter sat down."

CLOUTRAGE *(CLOWT-rage), n.*

Indignation of the insufficiently kowtowed to.

"As he watched his boss's ears turn pinkish when he learned he was to be put in a cheaper hotel than the other executives, Niles knew, as his long-suffering assistant, he'd hear at least three hours of cloutrage."

CUBICULL *(KEW-buh-KUL), n., v.*

Laying off of staff.

"Dawn looked with horror at the 'efficiency expert' they were introducing to the staff—it was clear that a major cubicull loomed."

DONELY *(DOAN-lee), adj.*

Having to finish something entirely by yourself.

"While donely Elspeth toiled away in the half-lit office, she knew her lazy coworkers were getting bombed at the Christmas party."

FAULTITASK *(FALL-tee-task), v.*

Mess up by trying to do too many things at once.

"Pierre's disastrous trip to the deck with a six-pack, two pizzas, the iPad, and their toddler was one of his wife's favorite tales of his faultitasking."

RESULTORY *(REH-zull-tuh-ree), adj.*

Utterly uninterested in outcomes.

"Orvil was the most resultory tennis player Orly had ever faced—once, she found him experimenting with how far he could hit a dandelion."

CHOREFUL *(CHORE-full), adj.*

Way too happy to work.

"David found his choreful sister bizarre, though he was happy to let her sweep up *and* load the dishwasher after dinner."

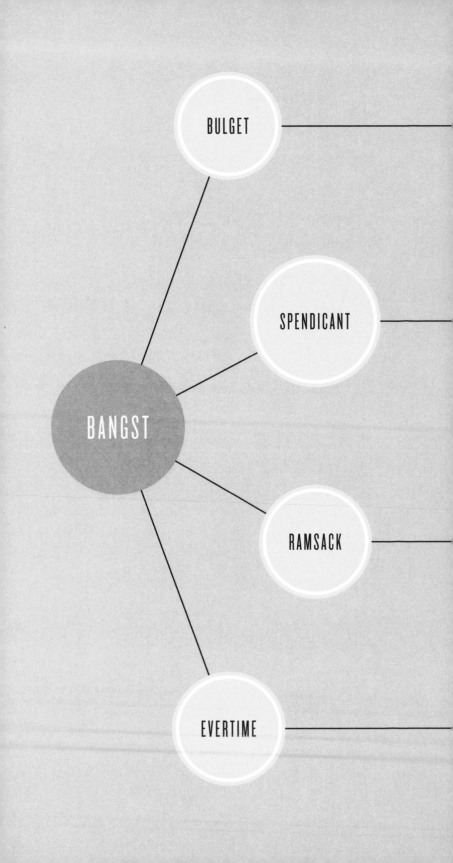

BULGET

SPENDICANT

BANGST

RAMSACK

EVERTIME

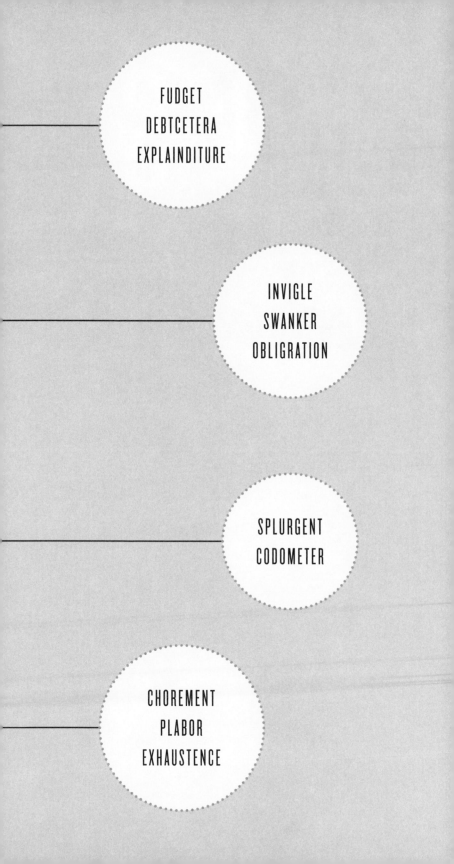

FUDGET
DEBTCETERA
EXPLAINDITURE

INVIGLE
SWANKER
OBLIGRATION

SPLURGENT
CODOMETER

CHOREMENT
PLABOR
EXHAUSTENCE

BANGST

(BANKST), n.

Stress over diminishing funds.

"Topher read the ATM printout carefully, filled with bangst. That couldn't be only two zeroes, could it?"

RAMSACK

(RAM-sak), n., v.

Online shopping spree.

"Barrie occasionally awoke to a browser filled with checkout pages from J. Crew, Amazon, and Athleta: She'd ramsacked the web again."

EVERTIME

(EH-ver-time), n.

Uninterrupted time on call.

"Nam never got paid extra for evertime, but the company had provided him two iPhones and even Google Glass to make sure he could never be AWOL."

BULGET
(BULJ-it), n.

A rapidly expanding spending plan.

"Jaime allowed the caviar and Champagne to stay, but he trimmed foie gras and aged Asiago off the bulget without blinking an eye at the protests."

SPENDICANT

(SPEN-dih-kant), n.

Cheap-o mooch.

"It was ridiculous that the head of the lab, who brought in a million dollars in grants every year, was such a spendicant, but Jules and Fran had become used to getting stiffed on bringing him lunch."

FUDGET *(FUJ-it)*, *n.*

(Poorly) estimated expenses.

"Yun hoped his partner wouldn't notice a few missing items and hedged amounts on what had become one of his clumsier Halloween-costume fudgets."

DEBTCETERA *(det-SET-er-uh)*, *n.*

A fuzzy amount of money one owes.

"Armand noted that his bank account registered several checks, late fees, withdrawals, and various other debtcetera that he'd ignore again later."

EXPLAINDITURE

(ek-SPLANE-di-cher), *n.*

Buying something outside one's budget because it is too wonderful to pass up.

"Sasha knew the $354 Eva Zeisel sugar bowl would be a brutal explainditure, but it was worth the two hours she'd have to spend convincing her accountant that it was a bargain."

INVIGLE *(in-VIG-gull)*, *v.*

Seduce or trick into attending.

"After Chirlaine invigled her brother into helping her move by asking, 'What are you doing tomorrow?' without telling him why she wanted to know, he never fell for it again."

SWANKER *(SWANK-er)*, *n.*

Someone who insists on black tie.

"Lee avoided all his sister-in-law's parties: He didn't feel like renting a tux every other month for such a swanker."

OBLIGRATION

(ah-bluh-GRAY-shun), *n.*

Annoying task.

"Every year, Leonard signed up for the 2K charity run, forgetting that he would curse the obligration when he dutifully trained through the winter months."

SPLURGENT *(SPLERJ-ent), adj.*

Compelling one to snap up immediately.

"Adelaide actually had to force herself to go only to Marshall's and other lower-priced stores, knowing that anywhere fancy, splurgency would take over and she'd find herself kitted out in Prada."

CODOMETER *(koh-DOM-uh-ter), n.*

Display of discounts in tally.

"Sean became addicted to extreme couponing simply for the pleasure of watching the codometer beep downward on the register."

CHOREMENT

(CHORE-meant), n.

Being haunted by to-dos.

"Zubair signed up for a front-of-the-house shift in his second week of working his after-school restaurant gig, having found working the massive dishwasher a positive chorement."

PLABOR *(PLAY-ber), v., n.*

Working while on vacation.

"Despite Louise's theft of her plabor-friendly mother's BlackBerry, their trip to Yellowstone still somehow involved emails to an assistant in front of Old Faithful."

EXHAUSTENCE

(eks-AW-stints), n.

The state of always being tired.

"Contemplating her exhaustence, Willa considered which she hated more: the late-night idling of delivery trucks or her two-hour commute."

(FIJ-ih-tul), adj.

Excessively checking one's devices.

"Victoria grew tired of watching her fidgital fiancé glance at his iPhone every five seconds."

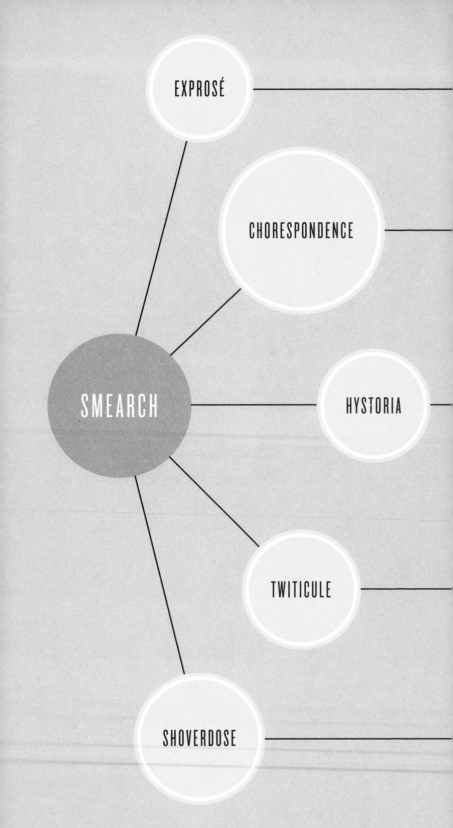

SMEARCH

EXPROSÉ

CHORESPONDENCE

HYSTORIA

TWITICULE

SHOVERDOSE

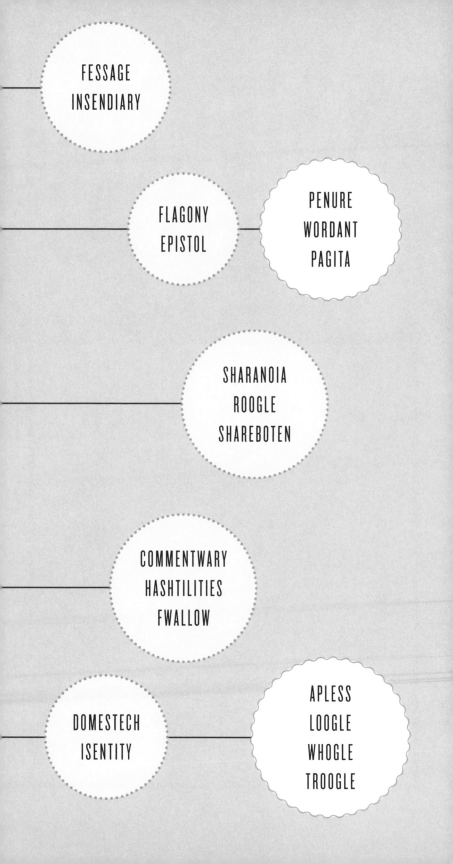

FESSAGE
INSENDIARY

FLAGONY
EPISTOL

PENURE
WORDANT
PAGITA

SHARANOIA
ROOGLE
SHAREBOTEN

COMMENTWARY
HASHTILITIES
FWALLOW

DOMESTECH
ISENTITY

APLESS
LOOGLE
WHOGLE
TROOGLE

SMEARCH

(SMURCH), v.

Google someone in hopes of finding bad news.

"'Never smearch an old rival, lest ye find them having received a MacArthur the year you lost your job,' became Matt's motto, for obvious reasons."

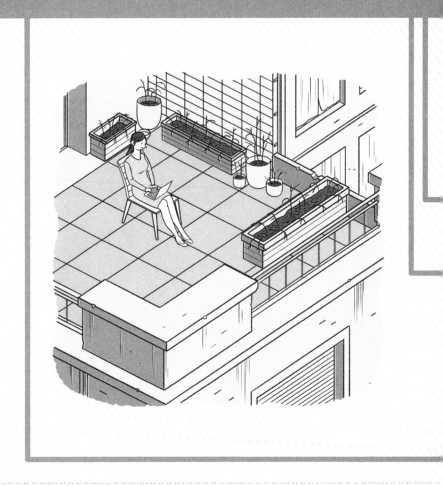

CHORESPONDENCE

(*chore-es-PAWN-dents*), *n.*

Mail you don't want to deal with.

"Emails from friends; health-care forms; eBay feedback—would Davida's chorespondence ever end?"

FLAGONY (*FLAG-uh-nee*), *n.*

Guilt over unanswered important emails.

"Consumed with flagony, Alec considered the last act of those who are overloaded with hundreds of actually 'Important' messages: declaring 'inbox bankruptcy' and deleting them all."

TWITICULE (*TWIT-i-kewl*), *v.*

Make fun of someone on Twitter.

"Clara thought the #sad hashtag attached to her article's link meant people were sharing pain about her failed roof garden, until she realized it was twiticule meant to break the news that her entire life was really lame."

EXPROSÉ *(eks-proh-ZAY), n., v.*

Message inadvertently sent to the one about whom you were complaining, or to send such a message.

"Susan was terribly embarrassed by her exprosé to her now-ex-friend until she realized all she'd done was make her life better by ridding herself of interminable brunches."

EPISTOL *(eh-PISS-tul), n.*

One who fires off messages.

"Yolande was the best epistol in the office—she could fill up her assistant's inbox in ten minutes flat."

HYSTORIA *(hiss-TORE-ee-uh), n.*

Panic if one second of life is not documented.

"When Nelson bought a second camera to make sure his guide could take pictures while he uploaded the files to Facebook, he realized he was suffering from hystoria."

FESSAGE *(FES-ij), n.*

An apologetic epistle.

"The housesitter texted Ella a fessage after first claiming, as he handed over the keys, that the wind must have knocked over her grandmother's ashes."

INSENDIARY

(in-SEN-dee-air-ee), n., adj.

Explosive communication.

"Marc started to pick up the phone to talk to his contractor, lest their online convos devolve yet again to a volley of ALL-CAPS insendiaries."

PENURE *(PEN-yer), n.*

The time before finishing a piece of necessary writing.

"Anne had 36 student evaluations to finish, and she took a swig of whiskey and began: Otherwise, she'd spend the vacation in penure."

WORDANT *(WERD-int), adj.*

Spilling over with words.

"Minimalist writer Jowita was amused to find her teenager rebelling by adoring the wordant geniuses of the age, from James Baldwin to Henry James to Joyce Carol Oates."

PAGITA *(PAH-ji-tuh), n.*

The stress of the unread.

"Roderick stared desperately at the stack of *New Yorker*s before he went on his business trip, trembling with pagita."

SHARANOIA

(SHARE-uh-NOY-uh), n.

Fear of what people are thinking of your posts.

"Even though she had only 72 friends, Irina suffered from such sharanoia that she often deleted her updates before people even responded."

ROOGLE *(ROOG-ul), n.*

Regret of a search.

"Samir stepped away from the computer filled with roogle. He hadn't needed to know his new boss was a Civil War reenactor."

SHAREBOTEN

(share-BOH-ten), adj.

Not to be posted on social media.

"The pregnancy was apparently shareboten until three months, although Serina's 'Dead rabbit!' Gmail status kind of gave it away."

COMMENTWARY

(COM-en-tware-ee), adj.

Worried about posting in case a million people respond.

"Newt was too commentwary to add his opinion to Dahlia's Facebook thread: He was sure to be tackled by every other responder."

HASHTILITIES

(hash-TIL-uh-tees), n.

Twitter fights.

"As Joyce wrote yet another cryptic statement, the hashtilities grew: One person tweeted that she couldn't mean it; another, she would never buy any of her novels; and a website published an entire article on why she should cancel her account."

FWALLOW *(FWAH-loh), v.*

Worry about who's defriended or unfollowed you.

"Lauren uninstalled the apps that let her know who'd defriended, blocked, and stopped sharing her updates. She was fwallowing again."

SHOVERDOSE

(SHOW-ver-dose), v.
To binge-watch a TV series.

"The couch was littered with Frito detritus,
a laptop opened to the Wiki for *Game of
Thrones*, and a set of fuzzy socks, while a
Roku screensaver bounced on the TV: Clearly,
Allison had been shoverdosing again."

DOMESTECH *(doh-MESS-tek), n.*

Responsible for family computer.

"As the resident domestech, Rose was responsible for defragmenting the drives, programming the router, and explaining to her parents why Gmail wasn't *really* free."

ISENTITY *(eye-SENT-ih-tee), n.*

Online persona.

"On dial-up, Prospera's screen name had conveyed a demure isentity, but by the era of Facebook and Twitter, her avatar was a daily shot of her morning bedhead."

APLESS *(APP-liss), adj.*

Lost without one's device.

"When her iPhone fell into a swamp, Melissa wandered around Tampa aplessly, unable to even call up Yelp's highest-rated restaurant."

LOOGLE *(LOO-gull), v.*

Search for bathroom online.

"When Erin became pregnant, she bought a smartphone entirely so she could loogle her way around when she traveled for work."

WHOGLE *(HOO-gull), v.*

Look up person online.

"'You can whogle me all you want,' laughed the philosophy professor to his freshman class. 'I scrubbed my online identity to freak out you nosy ingrates years ago.'"

TROOGLE *(TROO-gull), v.*

Use search engine to resolve a factual dispute.

"'Stop troogling me,' Andriana snapped. 'Warren Beatty was the goddamn love interest in *Splendor in the Grass*!'"

(HOME-en-clay-chur), n.

Real-estate lingo.

"If Sheba heard a real estate agent say 'open concept,' 'bonus room,' or 'perfect for entertaining' one more time, she was going to ban homenclature from her showings entirely."

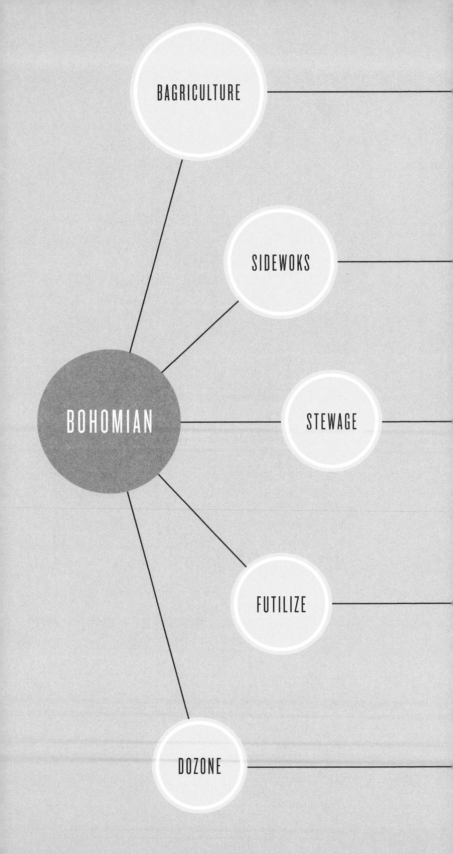

BAGRICULTURE

SIDEWOKS

BOHOMIAN

STEWAGE

FUTILIZE

DOZONE

CARSIMONY
BOUGHTHENTICITY

CLOSTER
TRINQUISITION
TROVEL

SHAMBULATE
SWEATHER

UMIGRATE
CLOGIN
THERMOSTATE
FROSTAGE

STINKUBUS
GERMAMENT

RUINSTALL
RUINFORCE

NAPT
DREAMISS

DROAM
FLYBERNATE

BOHOMIAN

(buh-HOME-ee-un), n., adj.
One who likes unconventional digs.

"Long-time bohomians, Mick and Marn had lived in a yurt, a shipping-container house, a church basement, and, finally, the edgiest of all: a redbrick Colonial in Rye."

FUTILIZE

(FEW-tul-ize), v.
Unsuccessfully try to figure out how to operate something.

"The counter was ridden with objects Amiya had futilized: a German juicer; two egg cups; the coveted Rabbit corkscrew."

DOZONE

(DOH-zohn), n.
Place that puts you to sleep.

"Dominique envied her brother, for whom the car was a dozone. For her it was a torment."

BAGRICULTURE

(BAG-rih-kul-chur), n.

The practice of saving shopping sacks to be environmental.

"Christine was an avid bagriculturist, keeping sacks from Whole Foods, Duane Reade, and even an obscure sandwich shop from a long-ago business trip, under the sink."

RUINSTALL *(roo-in-STAHL), v.*

Break while trying to put together.

"Lizzie invariably ruinstalled the notoriously buggy iTunes update right before a deadline, thereby knocking out her computer when she needed it most."

RUINFORCE *(roo-in-FORS), v.*

Destroy while trying to stabilize.

"With a jar of superglue, a nail gun, and a tube of wood filler, Faro ruinforced their kitchen table beyond repair."

SIDEWOKS

(SIDE-woks), n.

Circles of gum baked into pavement.

"Jessica tried to believe that Rosalie had never created one of the sidewoks defacing their path to the subway, but her incessant gum-chewing made it seem unlikely."

CARSIMONY *(car-suh-MOAN-ee), n.*

Having a small car or using it seldom.

"Hortense lamented her boyfriend's carsimony—if he had his way, they'd be driving a golf cart and not their Aspire through downtown."

BOUGHTHENTICITY

(BAW-then-tiss-it-ee), n.

Noncommercial lifestyle nonetheless acquired primarily through purchases.

"Paolo kicked back on his hand-hewn rocker while Irene proffered her collection of traditional trucker headwear—they were in a battle of boughthenticity for the ages."

STEWAGE *(STOO-ij), n.*

Garbage left out in heat.

"You could not get a MRSA from the city's odoriferous stewage, Jeffy was sure, but that didn't stop him from wearing rubber boots in August while in midtown."

CLOSTER *(CLAW-stur), v.*

Put in a safe spot and therefore make unfindable.

"It took Louise three years to realize she'd clostered her diamond earrings in a paper bag under the sink."

TRINQUISITION

(trin-kwiz-ISH-un), n.

Attempt to remember where one has left jewelry.

"Heartbroken, Tim abandoned the trinquisition on his father's lost cufflinks, which surfaced three years later in the pockets of a now way-too-small suit."

TROVEL *(TROH-vul), v.*

To travel with items that feel like home.

"Aurora thought it was insane for Angel to trovel with their grandmother's fine china, but Angel justified it by insisting that hotel plates were covered with bacteria."

SHAMBULATE
(SHAM-bew-late), v.

To fake speeding up while crossing street.

"Tariq gunned his Porsche at yet another dude shambulating in the crosswalk after the red light."

SWEATHER
(SWEH-thur), n.

Days that swing back and forth between hot and cold.

"The worst thing about spring sweather was arriving at work sopping wet and shivering your way home after five, Marian thought."

STINKUBUS *(STIN-kew-bus), n.*

Source of a mysterious stench.

"Niles finally realized the stinkubus in his kitchen was a sackful of rotting kale."

GERMAMENT *(JERM-uh-mint), n.*

The o'erhanging galaxy of contagions.

"Josh finally had to take a low dose of antianxiety medicine to quell his alarm and stop fixating on the window-placed crib's germament."

NAPT *(NAPT), adj.*

Falling asleep anywhere.

"Todd was almost embarrassingly napt, dropping off during a 15-minute bus ride and arriving home completely refreshed."

DREAMISS *(dree-MISS), adj.*

Failing to do something in a dream.

"Awake, Adelle had her pencils sharpened and her wristwatch tuned to the second, but at night she was sorely dreamiss, showing up four hours late to her S.A.T.s, often in her underwear."

DROAM *(DROME), v.*

To travel far in a dream.

"In real life, Zulina lived in a fifth-floor walk-up. At night, though, she droamed far and wide—teahouses in Prague; New Zealand crags; even, wearing wings, at a 20-story Nordstrom."

FLYBERNATE *(FLIE-burn-ate), v.*

To put oneself into deep sleep while on a plane.

"Shannon had found that if she got the earplugs and neck donut on before they even taxied, she could flybernate without interruption up to the descent."

THAT SHOULD BE A WORD

UMIGRATE *(UM-ih-grayt), v.*

Walk into room and realize one has no idea why one went there.

"Martha finally started jotting on her palm what she wanted in the other room: If she umigrated downstairs one more time, she was going to wear out the staircase treads."

CLOGIN *(CLOG-in), n.*

Person who blocks the way while checking device.

"When she first moved to the city, Docia would tap clogins at the subway exit politely—but after three months she just pushed them aside like everyone else."

THERMOSTATE *(THURM-oh-state), v.*

Insist that someone cannot be hot or cold.

"Although Olivia thermostated her wife could not possibly be cold, Suki took one look at the wide-open window in December and firmly slammed it down."

FROSTAGE *(FROSS-tij), adj.*

Imprisoned by cold.

"The winter of 2013–2014 held the entire East Coast frostage while blazing a terrifying trail of fires through the West."

(me-SPOHK), *adj.*

Tailored to one's lifestyle.

"Dylan was a member of the mespoke generation: From his iPod playlist to his Netflix choices to his favorite shot of espresso at his neighborhood café, he never had to experience anything that wasn't his explicit choice."

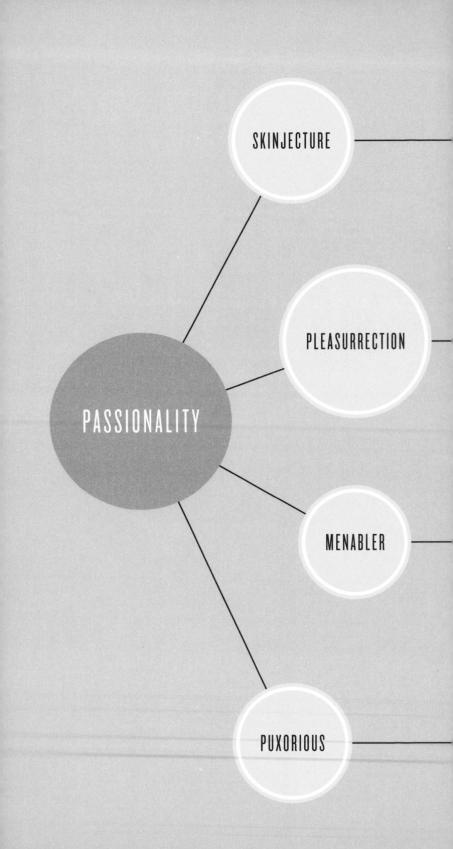

PASSIONALITY

SKINJECTURE

PLEASURRECTION

MENABLER

PUXORIOUS

ICONOPLAST
DONION
BORGEOUS
CLIPSTER

SHRINKLE
SMILEAGE
PRIMPLE
WRANKLE
PERIWRINKLE

FANALYST
FANECDOTE

MENITALIA
MENOPOLY
RUINVENT
CONSWERVATIVE

PURRIAH

PASSIONAL

(pash-un-AL-uh-tee), n.

Love for a foreign culture.

"Juan launched the day with the BBC World Service, a scone, and some PG tips he'd picked up on a recent trip: Since a year abroad at Oxford, he'd embraced his UK passionality."

ITY

SKINJECTURE
(skin-JEK-cher), n.
Speculation about plastic surgery someone's had.

"José loved lunching at the Beverly Wilshire: Eye job? Chin insert? Facial resurfacing? It was a festival of skinjecture."

MENABLER
(men-ABE-ler), n.

One who aids the patriarchy.

"If the CEO menabled Priya's favorite assistant, Dan, one more time by letting him speak over her in meetings, she was going to cough so loudly no one would hear him anyway."

PUXORIOUS
(pugs-ZOR-ee-us), adj.

Being overly fond of one's dog.

"Garp switched cafés after two puxorious owners allowed their pets to actually fight over a piece of bacon he'd unintentionally dropped."

PLEASURRECTION

(pleh-zhur-EK-shun), n.

Gladness that one you thought was dead is alive.

"Seeing his childhood rock idol on Twitter, Bruce was filled with pleasurrection—maybe the rest of the band hadn't died, either!"

FANALYST *(FAN-uh-list), n.*

One who dissects celebrity behavior.

"Imogene was the original fanalyst—she had been decoding celebs' body language practically since the advent of the talkies."

FANECDOTE *(FAN-ek-doht), n.*

Tale of encountering a celebrity.

"Barbara's favorite fanecdote was the time Mark Wahlberg gave her the eye in Union Square in 1997, but she now realized he was probably nearsighted."

MENITALIA *(men-ih-TAIL-ee-uh), n.*

A country in which men tell everyone what to do with their own genitalia.

"Karen couldn't believe that a retrogressive Congress was creating a menitalia of the U.S. that rivaled countries that sold off 12-year-old girls as brides."

MENOPOLY *(men-OP-uh-lee), n.*

An institution or market that is exclusively male.

"'Men look at a menopoly and they see a meritocracy,' Laura joked, showing Georgia the all-male newsroom."

RUINVENT *(roo-in-VENT), v.*

Revamp oneself for the worse.

"Joe Namath was ruinvented as an underwear salesman, thereby driving all athletic heroes straight into the cereal market."

CONSWERVATIVE
(con-SWERVE-uh-tiv), n.

One who tacks left when convenient.

"A long-time conswervative may have lost his touch when he railed against 'those people,' then hailed himself as 'a representative of the people' all in the same week."

ICONOPLAST (eye-KON-oh-plast), n.

One who refuses to get plastic surgery.

"Mary took heat from her friends for being an iconoplast, but she thought it was insane for them to risk death to take three inches off the midsection."

DONION (DUN-yun), n.

One who had too many face-lifts.

"Ned loved his actor son enough that when Rodney became such a donion he barely recognized him, he just told him he looked ten years younger."

BORGEOUS (BORE-jis), adj.

Showing cookie-cutter beauty.

"Portia had a parade of borgeous boyfriends, each one with the same dimple, wavy hair, crooked grin, and gently aged jeans."

CLIPSTER (KLIP-stir), n.

One who expresses coolness primarily through facial hair.

"Emily refused to give the clipster her number until he explained his handlebar moustache."

SHRINKLE *(SHRIN-kill)*, v.

Use Botox, etc.

"Stan's best friend, Ed, had shrinkled his face so thoroughly that he looked like he'd been rendered in Claymation."

PURRIAH

(pur-EYE-ah), n.

One with too many cats.

"It took Mac two years to realize his neighbors refused his invitations to play pinochle because his four shrieking cats had rendered him a purriah."

SMILEAGE *(SMILE-idge), n.*

Smile lines.

"Mara hated her smileage until her granddaughter put her chubby hand on Mara's cheek and said she loved those lines the best."

PRIMPLE *(PRIM-pull), v.*

Attempt to hide a blemish.

"After a month spooning Frappuccinos every day and never washing off her makeup, Molly had to primple massively on the night of the prom."

WRANKLE *(RANK-ul), n.*

Frown line.

"Unlike his twin sister, who'd practiced yoga since the age of 14, Alton's face was a striated mass of wrankles from his years as a probate attorney."

PERIWRINKLE *(PAIR-ee-rin-kill), n.*

Beginning of a line.

"Jolie scanned her chest for periwrinkles. Had spending her childhood resisting using baby oil instead of suntan lotion been for naught?"